MW01128424

better together*

*This book is best read together, grownup and kid.

 akidsco.com

a
kids
book
about

a kids book about HUMANI-TARIANISM

by Shahd Alasaly

a
kids
book
about

Printed in the United States of America.

A Kids Book About books are available online: *akidsco.com*

To share your stories, ask questions, or inquire about bulk
purchases (schools, libraries, and nonprofits), please use
the following email address: *hello@akidsco.com*

Print ISBN: 978-1-958825-25-9
Ebook ISBN: 978-1-958825-26-6

Designed by Rick DeLucco
Edited by Emma Wolf

To my dearest mother, father, brother, and husband. You have always encouraged me to be my best self and never settle for less, and for that, I am forever grateful.

To my beautiful children, Jenna, Kareem, and Zade. You are the future, and I know you will go on to do great things and make the world a better place.

With love and gratitude,
Shahd

Intro

I remember sitting down with my 3 kids, wanting to inspire them to do something meaningful that would benefit others. As a parent, I realized that instilling a sense of humanitarianism in my kids was just as important as teaching them to be kind and respectful. That's why I decided to write this book on humanitarianism for kids. I wanted to create a tool that parents and caregivers could use to help foster important conversations about the impact of our actions and the importance of helping others.

Just like kindness, humanitarianism starts at home. Having these conversations with our kids helps create an environment that encourages empathy and compassion, which can lead to a ripple effect felt around the world.

Through the stories and examples shared in this book, I hope to inspire kids everywhere to become agents of positive change in their own communities and beyond. Thank you for joining me on this journey toward a more compassionate and empathetic world.

Hi there!

My name is Shahd
(pronounced sha-hĭd).

And I want to share
an exciting way to do
some good in the world.

Sometimes, we call this

HUMANITA

Other times it's called philanthropy, ch

ARIANISM.

arity, outreach, or showing compassion.

Humanitarianism is a way of thinking, speaking, and acting that is based on...

- being a kind person,

- volunteering in our communities,

- helping and respecting others,

- practicing empathy,

and so much more!

My story with humanitarianism starts in 2011, when people in the country of Syria marched in the streets and protested for their rights and freedoms.

They wanted democracy in their country, which resulted in a long civil war.

And this war displaced millions of people who had to flee the country to find refuge, or a safe place to live, somewhere else.

This created an opportunity for humanitarian organizations to help provide important things like housing, food, healthcare, and support to build a life in new places.

This also presented the opportunity for people everywhere to welcome their new neighbors.

For example, in the United States...

- Doctors provided free healthcare for those who couldn't pay for it.

- Teachers provided tutoring for refugees who couldn't speak English.

- Social workers provided support for people to work through difficult circumstances.

- Artists found creative ways to help reduce feelings of sadness and anxiety.

- Restaurant owners donated food to those in need.

- Kids made cards in their classrooms to welcome their new friends.

The list of people using their skills to make an impact is huge!

The story of the Syrian civil war impacted me because my family is Syrian, and this conflict affected my extended family and their home country in countless ways.

I wanted to do humanitarian work in order to make a positive difference.

My work background is in psychology and sociology, so I decided to create something that would help my refugee neighbors process what they'd been through.

I started a clothing line
which employs refugees who
have experience sewing
and making clothes.

This allowed them to provide for their families and reminded them that their work matters and their skills are valuable.

Making clothes was also a form of art therapy, which helped them share their feelings and struggles, and work toward something positive.

IT FELT GOOD TO HELP OTHERS,

and it made me happy to see
the impact of doing good
for those around me.

UPLIF
WAR
MEA
Humanitarianism also feels... POSI
EXC
PURPOSE
FUN,

TING, FULFILLING,
m, EMPOWERING,
NINGFUL, JOYFUL,
TIVE, REWARDING,
ITING, CREATIVE,
FUL, CONNECTED,
AND EMOTIONAL.

Humanitarians can be anyone, from volunteers to professionals, and can work as teachers, doctors, psychologists, social workers, chefs, and so much more.

They can be old.

They can be young.

They can live anywhere!

What connects humanitarians is
a deep empathy for the world they
live in and the people around them.

When someone is empathetic, they put themselves in someone else's shoes to better understand how they think, feel, and experience life.

Humanitarians believe it is
our responsibility to help people
where we can.

And it's a lot easier to help people when we take the time to really listen and learn from their journey.

In a community, people make friends and learn from each other.

This makes everyone feel valued, connected, and provides a sense of safety in belonging.

It's important to make friends with people from different backgrounds who speak different languages...

because it expands our minds
and helps us learn about new
traditions and cultures!

Community-building gives us
a new understanding of how
the world works and encourages
humanitarian efforts
all over the world.

And it also it also encourages humanitarianism right here in our own towns.

And that's something **EVERYONE** can be a part of.

Just so you know, humanitarians aren't always grownups.

YOU CAN BE ONE TOO!

And here's a few ideas
to help you get started.

GET
INVOLVED.

Respond to needs in your community by volunteering at a local food bank.

CONTRIBUTE.

Create care packages for houseless people in your community, and include things like...

snacks,

water bottles,

hand sanitizers,

toiletries (toothbrushes, toothpaste, toilet paper),

and notes of kindness.

GIVE AWAY.

Donate money, skills, and important items.

When communities donate resources like clothing and toys to those who need them, we can grow together.

SHARE.

You can share smiles and kind words wherever you go!

It's a humanitarian thing to focus your efforts on making other people feel good.

MAKE NEW HABITS.

Practice empathy by looking out for others who may need help or some encouragement.

Use your voice and tell a grownup if you notice another kid getting bullied or treated with unkindness.

EVERYONE CAN MA

KE A DIFFERENCE.

Small acts of kindness go a long way
and have a much bigger impact
than we realize.

Humanitarianism is about helping and caring for others, no matter who they are, where they come from, how old, or how young they are.

Kindness and empathy build more loving

communities with deeper connections.

By doing humanitarian work,

WE CAN ALL MAKE THE WORLD A BETTER PLACE.

Outro

As you come to the end of this book, I hope you and your kids feel inspired to make a positive impact in your communities and the world around you.

Within these pages, we have explored the importance of empathy, kindness, and community-building, as well as the many ways in which individuals can make a difference in the world through humanitarian efforts.

I hope you will continue to have open and honest conversations with your kids about the importance of helping others and creating a more just and equitable society. By instilling these values in your kids from a young age, you are creating a generation of socially responsible and compassionate people who will go on to make a positive impact on the world.

Remember, small acts of kindness and generosity can go a long way. Whether it's volunteering at a local charity, donating to a worthy cause, or simply spreading positivity and love in your community, every action counts—and anyone can do humanitarian work! Thank you for taking the time to educate and inspire the next generation of changemakers.

About The Author

Shahd has always had a passion for helping others and spreading love through community-building. Her dedication to these values led her to pursue a PhD and career in sociology and humanitarian work, where she focuses her research on ways to improve the lives of those around her.

Despite her busy schedule, Shahd prioritizes wellness and relaxation in her downtime, recognizing the importance of taking care of her mental and physical health. She enjoys curling up with a good book and getting lost in a compelling story, using this time to unwind and recharge. Balancing family, academia, and humanitarian work, she cherishes time spent with her husband and children, enjoying nature, volunteering, or unwinding at home.

bluemeetsblue.com

a kids book about BEING INCLUSIVE

by Ashton Mota & Rebekah Bruesehoff

a kids book about diversity

by Chernoia Gordon

a kids book about LEADERSHIP

by Orion Jean

a kids book about IMMIGRATION

by MJ Ca

a kids book about

SAFETY

by Soraya Sutherlin, CEM
in partnership with JUDY

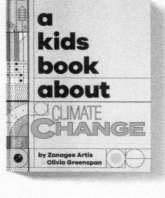

a kids book about CLIMATE CHANGE

by Zanagee Artis & Olivia Greenspan

a kids book about IMAGINATION

by LEVAR BURTON

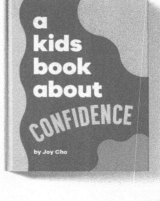

a kids book about CONFIDENCE

by Joy Cho

kids book about ANXIETY

Szabo
and Happy Faces

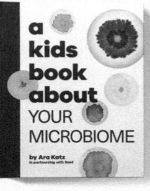

a kids book about YOUR MICROBIOME

by Ara Katz
in partnership with Seed

a kids book about racism

by Jelani Memory

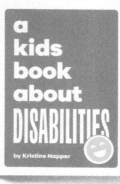

a kids book about DISABILITIES

by Kristine Napper

a kids book about bo

by KYLO

a kids book about DIVORCE

by Ashley Simpo

a kids book about cancer

by Dr. Kelsie Storm & Sarah Porter

a kids book about BEING TRANSGENDER

by Gia Parr
in partnership with The GenderCool Project

a kids book about DEPRESSION

by Kileah McIlvain

kids ook bout ame

a kids book about THE TULSA RACE MASSACRE

CPSIA information can be obtained
at www.ICGtesting.com
Printed in the USA
LVHW071915090523
746545LV00004B/12

9 781958 825259